FOLENS IDEAS BANK
MATERIALS AND CHANGE

Godfrey Hall

Contents

How to use this book	2	Sieves	26
Introduction	3	Separating and purifying	28
Everyday materials	4	Separating a mixture	30
Materials and their uses	6	Solid, liquid and gas	32
Plastics	8	Change of state	34
Fabrics	10	Insulation	36
Metals	12	Melting chocolate	38
Rust	14	Cooking an egg	40
Decay	16	Candle change	42
Rocks	18	Cooking	44
Concrete	20	Assessment	46
Solubility	22	Eight ways to help ...	48
Evaporation	24		

Folens Publishers

How to use this book

Ideas Bank books provide ready-to-use, practical, photocopiable activity pages for children, **plus** a wealth of ideas for extension and development.

TEACHER IDEAS PAGE

Suggestions for developing work on the photocopiable pages.

Clear focus to the activity.

Everyday context.

Background information for teachers.

Suggestions for assessment.

Extension activities suggested to take the work one stage further.

PHOTOCOPIABLE ACTIVITY PAGE

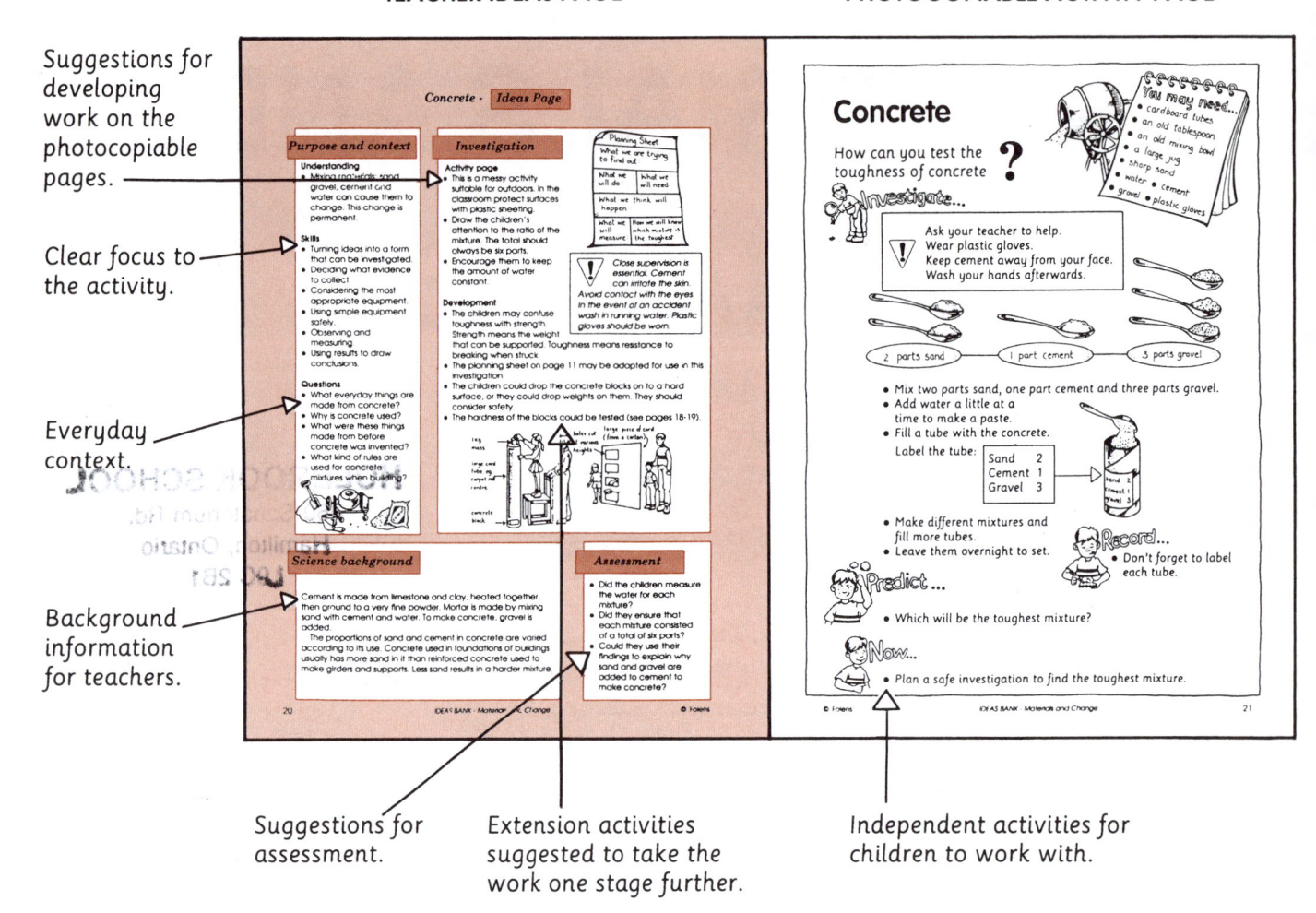

Independent activities for children to work with.

- Time-saving, relevant and practical, **Ideas Bank** books ensure that you will always have work ready to hand.

Folens books are protected by international copyright laws. All rights reserved. The copyright of all materials in this book, except where otherwise stated, remains the property of the publisher and author(s). No part of this publication may be reproduced, stored in a retrieval system, or transmitted, in any form or by any means, for whatever purpose, without the written permission of Folens Limited.

Folens do allow photocopying of selected pages of this publication for educational use, providing that this use is within the confines of the purchasing institution. You may make as many copies as you require for classroom use of the pages so marked.

This resource may be used in a variety of ways; however it is not intended that teachers or children should write into the book itself.

© 1995 Folens Limited, on behalf of the author.

Cover by: Design for Marketing, Ware.   Cover Photo: Zefa.

Illustrations by: Susan Hutchison.   Editor: Andy Bailey.   Layout Artist: Suzanne Ward.

First published 1995 by Folens Limited, Albert House, Apex Business Centre, Boscombe Road, Dunstable LU5 4RL, England.

ISBN 1 85276695-6

Printed in Singapore

Introduction

Ideas Bank: Materials and Change is designed to help busy teachers provide interesting and challenging scientific investigations. It recognises the growing demands placed on the teacher, particularly the non-specialist, in planning activities that promote children's learning in science.

Each activity sheet can be used to:

- support existing work
- stimulate further investigations
- introduce a new area of science

The photocopiable pages have been organised to take the children through a number of scientific investigations, at the same time fostering their interest in science. They are informative but essentially straightforward and fun to use.

Science is all about predicting, testing and drawing conclusions based on findings and previous experience. The children should be excited about what they are doing, but at the same time able to record their results clearly and accurately. If they are in doubt they should repeat their tests and make sure that they are completely fair.

It needs to be pointed out that tests sometimes fail or give inaccurate results and so it may be necessary to re-test. This should be built in as part of the scientific procedure and not seen by the children as a sign of failure. It may therefore be necessary to test several times, controlling the variables on each occasion.

When working together it is important that the children are able to question their findings and discuss possible outcomes. Discussion will help them consider a variety of ideas and options which they may not have thought of.

Children's ideas can often be based on preconceptions and so it is important that they should have the opportunity to investigate and discuss with others. Many children have certain ideas about scientific principles gleaned from a number of sources. Any challenge to these ideas needs to be backed up by practical demonstration or testing. Teachers may find that even after exhaustive practical work and testing pupils still cling on to their previous ideas.

Good questioning and well structured discussion should solve some of these problems. Some of the activity pages have been designed to allow the children to record directly on to the sheet whilst others will require a notebook.

There is a list of equipment required at the top of each of the activity pages. Additional suggestions and support can be found on the ideas pages. The assessment and recording sheets provide examples for teachers to adapt to suit the school's own record-keeping system.

Everyday materials - Ideas Page

Purpose and context

Understanding
- Materials can be grouped according to their characteristics.
- Some materials are natural and may be shaped or treated according to their uses. Others are manufactured.

Skills
- Making comparisons.
- Making observations.
- Using tables.

Questions
- How do ceramics differ from other materials?
- How are ceramics like each other?
- How do plastics differ from other materials?
- How are plastics like each other?

Ask similar questions about wood and textiles.
- Which materials are natural? (Which natural materials have been treated in some way?)
- Which materials have been manufactured?

Investigation

Activity page
- The collection of materials should include textiles, metals, plastics, ceramics, wood, paper, stone.
- Include cups and mugs, clothes, cork, earthenware, plastic and ceramic tiles, plant pots, drinks containers made from paper, card, plastic and metal.
- Encourage the children to sort the items according to what they observe about the material, not according to their use.
- Provide reference books for finding out about the sources of materials.
- Make lists of natural materials and objects made from them. See if the children can match them. This can be done using two sets of pictures.

Metals	Textiles	Ceramics	Plastics	Wood	Skins
teaspoon	T-shirt	mug	juice bottle	spoon	belt
beaker	skirt	plant pot	cola bottle		shoes
buckle	jeans	wall tile	shoes		
dessert spoon	tights	floor tile	floor tile		
drink can	pullover		raincoat		

Science background

Wood: feels hard and warm and is a poor conductor of heat. It makes a dull sound when struck or dropped.
Metals: feel hard and cold. They make a ringing sound when struck. Some can be made into sheets to make cans, parts of cars and so on. These are malleable metals and include aluminium and steel. Some can be drawn into wire. These are ductile and include copper and steel. Most metals can be cast to make, for example, buttons and coins. They are good conductors of heat and electricity.
Plastics: can be cast into moulds to make, for example, bottles and cups. Some plastics feel cold. Expanded polystyrene feels warm. It is a poor conductor of heat and so does not conduct heat from the hand.
Ceramics: are made from clay that has been fired. They feel cold and hard. They are fragile and do not bend.

Assessment

- Can the children sort the materials into groups that have particular characteristics?
- Can they describe these characteristics?
- Can they describe how they distinguish between materials?

Everyday materials

How can you sort and classify everyday materials **?**

You may need...
- a collection of spoons
- mugs, cups and beakers
- clothes, pebbles
- floor and wall coverings
- drinks containers
- plant pots

Investigate...

- Sort the materials into groups. Number the groups.
- Materials in a group must be like each other in at least one way.

! Take care with fragile materials.

Record...

- Describe how the materials in each group are like each other (their similarities).

Group	Similarities
1	
2	
3	
4	
5	
6	

Now...

- Find out more about the different types of materials.
- Make your own chart to sort them into metals, textiles, ceramics, plastics, wood, stone, skins or paper.

Materials and their uses - Ideas Page

Purpose and context

Understanding
- How materials are used in our everyday lives.
- What makes materials suitable for particular purposes.

Skills
- Making observations.
- Using tables.

Questions
- What materials can be used to make drainpipes?
- Why are these materials chosen?
- What are the advantages of each material?
- What can be used to make window frames?
- What are the advantages of each material?

Investigation

Activity page
- Ask the children to note where each material is used. Ask them what could have been used instead.
- Why do they think that particular material was chosen?

Development
- Make a collection of materials that are used for specific jobs, such as paper for writing on and wood for making furniture.
- Ask the children to list the materials used to make everyday objects used at home. They could note the advantages and disadvantages of the materials for these uses.

Object	Material	Advantages	Disadvantages
saucepan	metal	conducts heat, does not break when dropped	dents easily
spoon	wood	does not conduct heat easily	difficult to clean
spoon	plastic	does not scratch non-stick pans	melts when hot

Science background

The characteristics of a material depend on the ways in which its particles (atoms and molecules) are joined.

Wood
Plant cells are made largely of cellulose, which has long chain-like molecules bonded together at intervals.

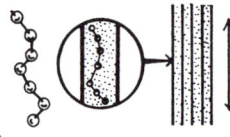

Metals
Metals are crystalline: their atoms are arranged in symmetrical patterns. This is altered when alloys are made, producing a different symmetrical arrangement.

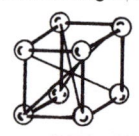

Rubber
Rubber molecules are arranged in long chains tangled together.

Plastics
Most plastics are made from petroleum products, whose carbon and hydrogen atoms are organised in a chain-like arrangement.

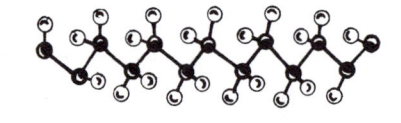

Assessment

- Can the children distinguish between natural and manufactured materials?
- Can they explain why particular materials are used for certain jobs?
- Can they list the advantages and disadvantages of using plastics and iron/steel to make drainpipes and gutters; plastics, iron/steel, aluminium and wood for window frames?

Materials and their uses

You may need...
- a clipboard
- your teacher's permission to look around the school

How are materials chosen for making everyday objects **?**

Investigate...

- Look around the school and see if you can spot how these materials are being used.

Record...

Material	Use
Wood	
Metals	
Textiles	
Ceramics	
Plastics	
Rubber	
Stone	
Paper	

Now...

- Choose six objects from your list and explain why they are made from that material. What else could they be made from?

© Folens — IDEAS BANK - Materials and Change

Plastics - Ideas Page

Purpose and context

Understanding
- The characteristics of plastics.
- How the uses of plastics are related to their characteristics.

Skills
- Using simple equipment.
- Making observations.
- Using tables.
- Using results to draw conclusions.
- Obtaining information from first-hand sources.

Questions
- Which everyday objects could NOT be made from plastics? Why not?
- Were you surprised that any of the objects you found were made from plastics? Why?

Investigation

⚠ *Take care with falling weights.*

Activity page
- Provide a range of everyday objects made from as many different types of plastics as possible (see Science background).

- The children should find that plastics can be transparent, translucent or opaque. They can be coloured. Not all plastics float. Some soften in hot water. All are waterproof. Some are more brittle than others. Some are more flexible than others.

Development
- Can the children think of a way to test the strength of plastic sheeting cut from carrier bags?

Plastic sample	Weight needed to break it
1	250g
2	60g
3	600g

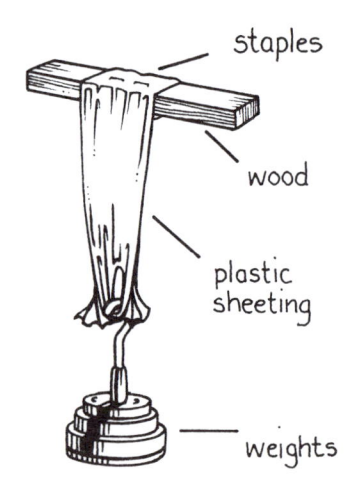

Science background

Plastics are polymers (poly = many, meris = parts). Their molecules form long chains, sometimes consisting of thousands of units (see page 6).

Some plastics soften in heat. These are thermoplastic. Thermosetting plastics harden and remain rigid in heat. There are many forms of plastics, including acrylics, bakelite, celluloid, cellulose, acetate, epoxy resins, nylon, polyesters, polycarbonate, polyethylene (polythene), polypropylene, polystyrene, PTFE (polytetrafluorethylene), polyurethane, PVC (polyvinylchloride).

Assessment

- Can the children explain how plastics are alike?
- Can they identify the observable differences between different plastics?
- Can they explain how plastics are different from other materials?
- Can they explain what makes plastics suitable for particular uses?

Plastics

What is special about plastics?

You may need...
- a collection of plastic objects
- a bowl of very warm water (not hot enough to scald you)
- scissors or safety snips
- a tank of cold water
- a dropper

Investigate...

- Test each plastic object.

- Hold it in front of a light. 
- Twist it. 
- Squash it. 
- Put it into water. 
- Heat it. 
- Drop water on it.

Record...

- Record your findings on this chart:

Plastic object	Transparent, translucent or opaque	Could be twisted	Could be squashed	Floated	Conducted heat	Waterproof

Interpret...

- How are plastics similar to each other?
- How are they different from other materials?

© Folens   IDEAS BANK - Materials and Change

Fabrics - Ideas Page

Purpose and context

Understanding
- Comparing fabrics on the basis of their properties.
- How the uses of fabrics are related to their characteristics.

Skills
- Planning investigations.
- Using predictions to aid planning.
- Fair testing.
- Selecting and using equipment.
- Recording measurements.
- Using tables and graphs.
- Evaluating the validity of a question.

Questions
- What do you notice about the fabrics used to make overalls, party clothes, sportswear?
- Which fabric is most often used in making overalls?
- Which fibres are natural and which are manufactured?

Investigation

Activity page
- Provide a selection of fabrics, including some that are very hardwearing: heavy duty denim, canvas, sailcloth, cotton, nylon, silk, acrylic, wool, linen.
- The children could test each fabric by wrapping it around a wooden block and rubbing it on a rough surface, such as concrete or asphalt.
- They could count how many 'rubs' it takes to make a hole in each fabric.
- To make the test fair they should make each rub the same length.
- They could record their findings on a graph.

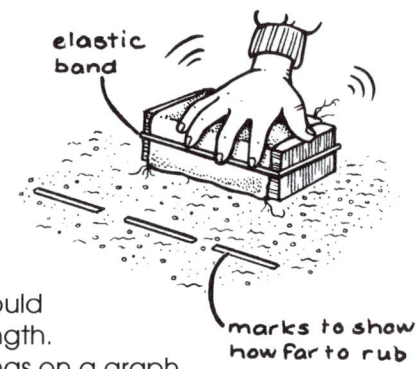

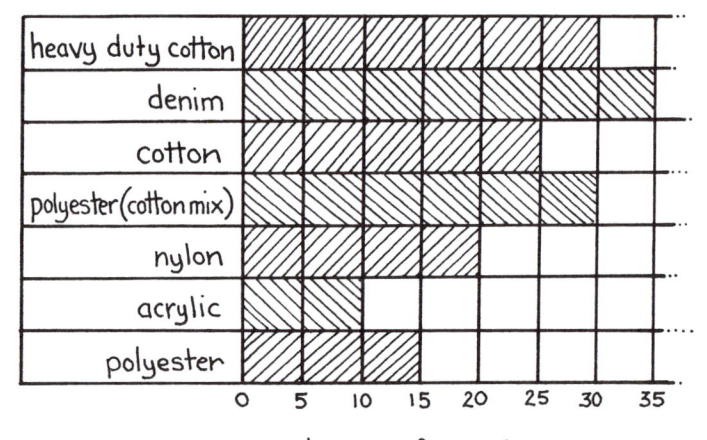

Science background

Natural fibres include cotton, wool, silk and linen (from flax). Synthetic fibres can be obtained as a by-product of petrochemicals. There are a number of fibres that can now be obtained from wood. Hardwearing does not mean strong. Strong fabrics are those that can support the greatest weight without tearing.

Assessment

- Did the children identify the variables in their investigation? For example, how hard they rubbed the fabric and the length of each 'rub'.
- Was the test 'fair'.
- Did the children repeat their investigations when necessary to ensure valid results?
- Did they ask questions when they conducted their tests?

IDEAS BANK - Materials and Change

Fabrics

How can you test fabrics to find out how hardwearing they are **?**

You may need...

Investigate... What we will do.

What we will keep the same for each fabric.

What we will measure.

How we will know which fabric is the toughest.

Predict... Our predictions.

Our findings.

Interpret... What we have found out.

Now... How we could improve our test.

Metals - Ideas Page

Purpose and context

Understanding
- The characteristics of metals.
- Differences between metals.

Skills
- Using simple equipment.
- Making observations and measurements.
- Using tables to present results.
- Using results to draw conclusions.

Questions
- Which everyday objects are made from metal?
- What are the advantages of these metals?
- What are their disadvantages?
- Why is electrical wiring made from metal?

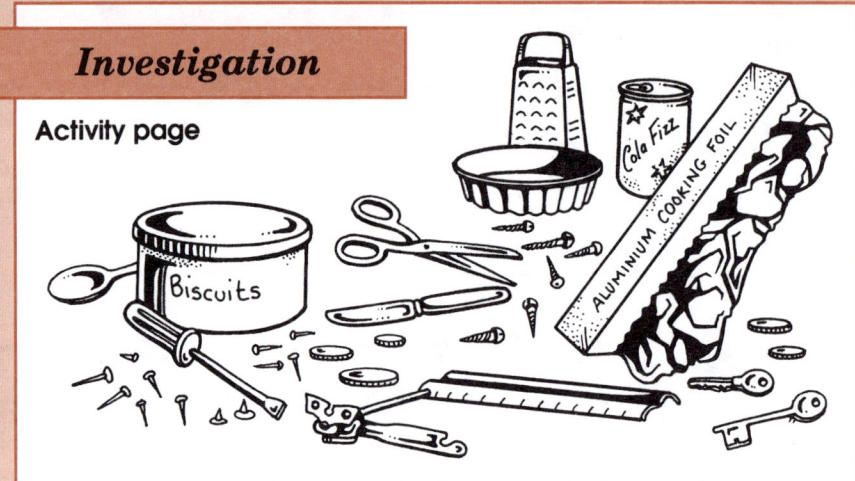

Investigation

Activity page

- Collect and display everyday items made from metal.
- Ask the children to write their own definitions of 'metal'.

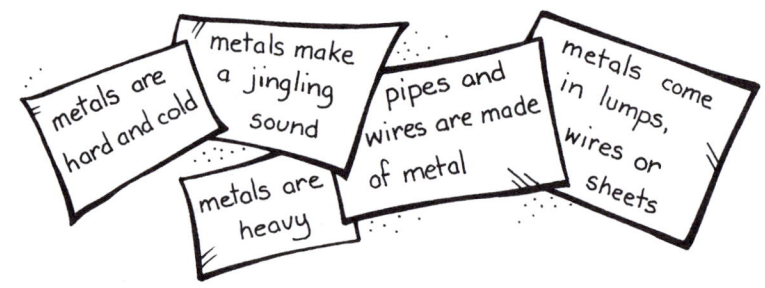

metals are hard and cold
metals make a jingling sound
pipes and wires are made of metal
metals come in lumps, wires or sheets
metals are heavy

- The children will need to know how to make a simple circuit with a gap.
- Provide a set of labelled metal samples, obtainable from educational suppliers.
- For the second part of the investigation the children will need the same set of samples, but not labelled.

Science background

The majority of metals found in the Earth's crust are ores. Metals are extracted from the ore by smelting when the ore is heated to very high temperatures or by electrolysis.

Metals are hard, shiny, strong, not easily broken when pulled (high tensile strength), dense, have a colour, feel cold, make a musical note when struck (sonorous) and are good conductors of heat and electricity.

Copper is used for producing electrical wires and cables. Alloys are produced by combining metals. For example, brass is an alloy of copper and zinc.

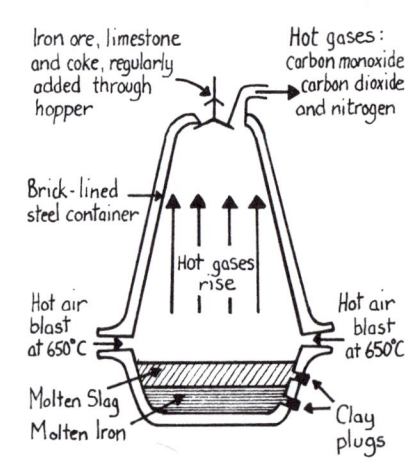

Iron ore, limestone and coke, regularly added through hopper
Hot gases: carbon monoxide, carbon dioxide and nitrogen
Brick-lined steel container
Hot gases rise
Hot air blast at 650°C
Molten Slag
Molten Iron
Clay plugs

Extracting iron from iron ore.

Assessment

- Ask the children to write their definitions of metals.
- They could compare these with their earlier ideas.
- How have their ideas changed?
- Do the children know that metals are good conductors of electricity?
- Do they know which metals are magnetic?

IDEAS BANK - Materials and Change

Metals

What are the differences and similarities between metals ?

You may need...
- a set of labelled metal samples
- a magnet
- a battery
- metal polish
- wire
- crocodile clips
- a bulb in a holder
- a screwdriver

Investigate...

- Test each metal sample. 
- Bend it. 
- Polish it. 
- Touch it with a magnet. 
- Put it across a gap in a circuit. 
- Drop it on a hard surface.

Record...

- Record your observations on this chart:

Metal	Colour	Bendy?	Will it shine?	Magnetic?	Does it conduct electricity?	Sound when dropped
Iron						
Steel						
Tinplate						
Aluminium						
Copper						
Brass						
Lead						

Now...

- Can you use your chart to identify unknown metals?

© Folens — IDEAS BANK - Materials and Change

Rust - Ideas Page

Purpose and context

Understanding
- Oxygen and water in the air are needed to make iron rust.
- Rust is one type of iron oxide.
- Rust can be prevented by protecting iron from contact with air and water.
- It is a chemical change.

Skills
- Making observations.
- Using tables to present results.
- Using results to draw conclusions.
- Relating results to predictions.
- Using observations to explain which metals rust and in what conditions.

Questions
- Which everyday objects have you seen with rust on them?
- What do you notice about painted iron and steel?
- Which metals do not seem to rust?

Investigation

Activity page
- The children should keep the jar that contains only dry air and the nail closed to prevent moisture entering.
- Use transparent plastic jars.
- If the nail that is completely covered with water does rust, this is because of air bubbles in the water.
- The children could work out and record the conditions needed to cause rust on iron or steel.

Did the nail rust?	
water	✗
air	✗
air and water	✓

Development
- Ask the children to experiment with reducing the amount of rust on the nail. This can be done by cutting down the amount of oxygen that reaches the nail by painting or covering it in grease. They could use petroleum jelly or non-toxic gloss paint.

⚠ Avoid solvent based varnishes.

- Once they have done this they can put the nail into water or bury it and compare their results with an uncoated nail.
- Test out a variety of other metals under water, for example aluminium, copper and zinc. How do they react under the same conditions? How do they change?

Science background

When iron or steel are exposed to oxygen and water they rust. Rust is iron oxide, produced when iron reacts with air or water. This can only be prevented by keeping air and water out.
Iron and steel may be protected by galvanising (coating in zinc), tin plating, painting, varnishing or coating with grease. Other metals oxidise in contact with air and water but their oxides do not corrode the metal, in fact they may even protect it:
Aluminium oxide – a whitish green coating that protects the metal.
Copper oxide – a green coating that protects the metal.

Assessment

- Could the children identify the conditions needed for rusting of iron (water and air)?
- Did they appreciate the need to keep the 'empty' jar closed and dry?
- Did they understand that the 'empty' jar contained air?

Rust

What makes iron rust ?

You may need...
- three new, shiny iron nails, with no rust
- three screw-topped plastic jars
- a plant spray
- water

Investigate...

- Spray a small amount of water in one jar.
- Fill another jar with water.
- Leave the third jar empty. Make sure it is dry.   
- Put a nail in each jar and put the lid on.
- Examine the nails each week.

Record...

- Record your observations on this chart:

Contents of jar	Observations			
	Week 1	Week 2	Week 3	Week 4
Air				
Air & water				
Water				

Interpret...

- What does your investigation tell you about rusting?

Now...

- Think of some ways to prevent a steel nail from rusting. Try them. Record your findings.

© Folens   IDEAS BANK - Materials and Change

Decay - Ideas Page

Purpose and context

Understanding
- Some materials decay when they are buried.
- Untreated organic (plant or animal) materials, such as leaves, wood and apple cores, decay more quickly than inorganic materials (for example, paper, cloth).
- Water and air cause decay, as do organisms living in the soil.

Skills
- Making observations.
- Using findings to draw conclusions.
- Using scientific observations to explain the uses of materials.

Questions
- Which everyday objects decay? Which do not?
- When is decay useful?
- When is it not useful?

Investigation

Activity page
- Prepare the children for a long-term investigation.
- If possible leave the materials longer than the eight weeks suggested.
- They may see very few changes after 1 week.
- Ask the children to use their findings to decide which items of household rubbish could be buried.

⚠ *Ensure that the children wear plastic gloves and wash their hands after the investigation.*

Rubbish	Will it decay when buried?
Yoghurt pot	No
Cling film	No
Tissue paper	Yes
Biscuit paper	Yes

- Investigate what is done with waste materials that do not decay.

Science background

When living things die and begin to decay they are attacked by bacteria and fungi. Some are initially broken down by scavengers such as sexton beetles. Earthworms may also feed on plant remains. During decay and decomposition any living tissues or once living tissues will be changed to humus, which in the end breaks down completely to form carbon dioxide, water and simple mineral salts.

Some materials will not break down completely but change in nature, for example a nail may become rusty. It will change in colour, turning brown, and the surface will change as the oxygen reacts with the water in the air to form iron oxide.

Assessment

- Did the children predict what would happen to the buried materials?
- Did their ideas change after the investigation?
- Did they record their findings carefully?
- What conclusions did they draw from their findings?
- Can they use their findings to explain which materials should not be used to make disposable items?

IDEAS BANK - Materials and Change

Decay

What happens to materials when they are buried underground **?**

You may need...
- paper • metal foil
- a plastic bag • nylon
- a leaf • cotton
- a plastic bowl or tank
- damp soil
- plastic gloves
- a small spade

Investigate...

- Bury each material in the soil.
- Dig them up and examine them after 1 week, 3 weeks, 8 weeks ...

Record...

- Record your findings on this chart:

Material	1 week	3 weeks	8 weeks
Paper			
Nylon			
Leaf			
Foil			
Plastic bag			
Cotton			

Interpret...

- Use your findings to explain which materials decay the quickest.

© Folens — IDEAS BANK - Materials and Change

Rocks - Ideas Page

Purpose and context

Understanding
- Comparing rocks on the basis of hardness.
- Relating the hardness of rocks to their everyday uses.

Skills
- Making observations.
- Using charts to represent results.
- Using results to draw conclusions.

Questions
- What is the softest thing you can think of?
- What is the hardest thing you can think of?
- What everyday things are made from rocks?

Investigation

Activity page
- Provide rocks that vary in hardness. If possible include flint and granite (both hard), limestone (softer), chalk and baked clay (soft).

Development
- Ask the children to think of a way to measure the hardness of rocks using 'scratchers' that become progressively harder: fingernail, paper clip, steel nail, nail file, carborundum block.
- Results could be recorded on a chart.

Streak test
- Another activity linked with the classification process can be carried out by rubbing each rock on the back of an unglazed tile. Different rocks make different marks. For example, malachite – green streak, galena – grey streak.

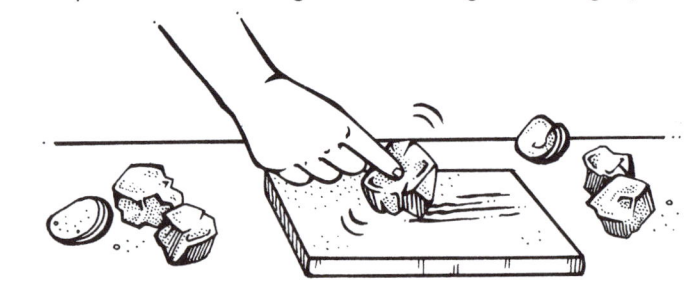

What scratched it?	Chalk	Granite
Fingernail	✔	✗
Paper clip	✔	✗
Nail file	✔	✗
Coin	✔	✗

Rock

Science background

Hardness should not be confused with strength. Strength means the force of compression or expansion that a material can support.

Hardness means ability to withstand abrasion. Mohs' scale of hardness relates to the hardness of minerals.

Mohs' scale of hardness			
1	talc	6	orthoclase
2	gypsum	7	quartz
3	calcite	8	topaz
4	fluorspar	9	corundum
5	apatite	10	diamond

Hardness Scale
The known hardness of everyday objects may help to measure the hardness of a rock.

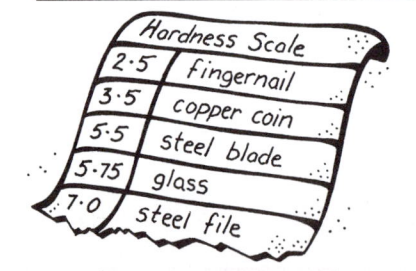

Hardness Scale
- 2·5 fingernail
- 3·5 copper coin
- 5·5 steel blade
- 5·75 glass
- 7·0 steel file

Assessment

- Did the children check that each scratch was really a scratch and not just bits of the other rock?
- Could they order the rocks from softest to hardest after the investigation?
- Can they think of a fair way to measure the hardness of rocks using any other material?

Rocks

How can you test rocks for hardness **?**

You may need...
- six small pieces of rock-all different
- a soft cloth
- a felt-tipped pen

Investigate...

- Number each rock sample.

- Scratch one rock with each of the others in turn.

- Rub the mark with a cloth.

If you can rub it off it is not a scratch, but bits that have rubbed off the other rock. If you cannot rub it off it is a scratch.

Record...

- Complete this chart to show which rock scratched which others.

	Samples tested					
Scratched by	1	2	3	4	5	6
1	▓					
2		▓				
3			▓			
4				▓		
5					▓	
6						▓

Interpret...

- Put your rock samples in order: softest ⟶ hardest

© Folens   IDEAS BANK - Materials and Change

Concrete – Ideas Page

Purpose and context

Understanding
- Mixing materials: sand, gravel, cement and water can cause them to change. This change is permanent.

Skills
- Turning ideas into a form that can be investigated.
- Deciding what evidence to collect.
- Considering the most appropriate equipment.
- Using simple equipment safely.
- Observing and measuring.
- Using results to draw conclusions.

Questions
- What everyday things are made from concrete?
- Why is concrete used?
- What were these things made from before concrete was invented?
- What kind of rules are used for concrete mixtures when building?

Investigation

Activity page
- This is a messy activity suitable for outdoors. In the classroom protect surfaces with plastic sheeting.
- Draw the children's attention to the ratio of the mixture. The total should always be six parts.
- Encourage them to keep the amount of water constant.

Development
- The children may confuse toughness with strength. Strength means the weight that can be supported. Toughness means resistance to breaking when struck.
- The planning sheet on page 11 may be adapted for use in this investigation.
- The children could drop the concrete blocks on to a hard surface, or they could drop weights on them. They should consider safety.
- The hardness of the blocks could be tested (see pages 18-19).

! Close supervision is essential. Cement can irritate the skin. Avoid contact with the eyes. In the event of an accident wash in running water. Plastic gloves should be worn.

Science background

Cement is made from limestone and clay, heated together, then ground to a very fine powder. Mortar is made by mixing sand with cement and water. To make concrete, gravel is added.

The proportions of sand and cement in concrete are varied according to its use. Concrete used in foundations of buildings usually has more sand in it than reinforced concrete used to make girders and supports. Less sand results in a harder mixture.

Assessment

- Did the children measure the water for each mixture?
- Did they ensure that each mixture consisted of a total of six parts?
- Could they use their findings to explain why sand and gravel are added to cement to make concrete?

Concrete

How can you test the toughness of concrete ?

You may need...
- cardboard tubes
- an old tablespoon
- an old mixing bowl
- a large jug
- sharp sand
- water
- cement
- gravel
- plastic gloves

Investigate...

⚠ Ask your teacher to help.
Wear plastic gloves.
Keep cement away from your face.
Wash your hands afterwards.

(2 parts sand) — (1 part cement) — (3 parts gravel)

- Mix two parts sand, one part cement and three parts gravel.
- Add water a little at a time to make a paste.
- Fill a tube with the concrete.
  Label the tube:

Sand	2
Cement	1
Gravel	3

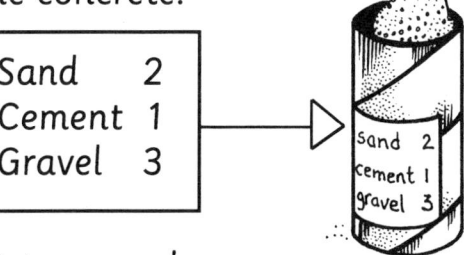

- Make different mixtures and fill more tubes.
- Leave them overnight to set.

Record...
- Don't forget to label each tube.

Predict...
- Which will be the toughest mixture?

Now...
- Plan a safe investigation to find the toughest mixture.

© Folens   IDEAS BANK - Materials and Change

Solubility - Ideas Page

Purpose and context

Understanding
- Some materials dissolve in water.
- The hotter the water the quicker they dissolve.
- Stirring speeds up dissolving.

Skills
- Saying whether the evidence collected supports any predictions made.
- Fair testing.
- Using predictions in planning an investigation.

Questions
- How can you tell when a material has dissolved?
- What do you see?
- What foods can you think of that dissolve?
- What foods do not dissolve?

Investigation

Activity page
- The children could try to find the 'record times' in which they can make each material dissolve (stirring more and more vigorously, using hotter water, within safety limits). They could record dissolving times against the temperature of the water used.
- Ask the children what it is about some substances that makes them dissolve more quickly, for example the size of the pieces different types of sugar. Ask them to fill a measuring jug with 200ml of hot water and see how many spoonfuls of salt they can add before the water becomes saturated.

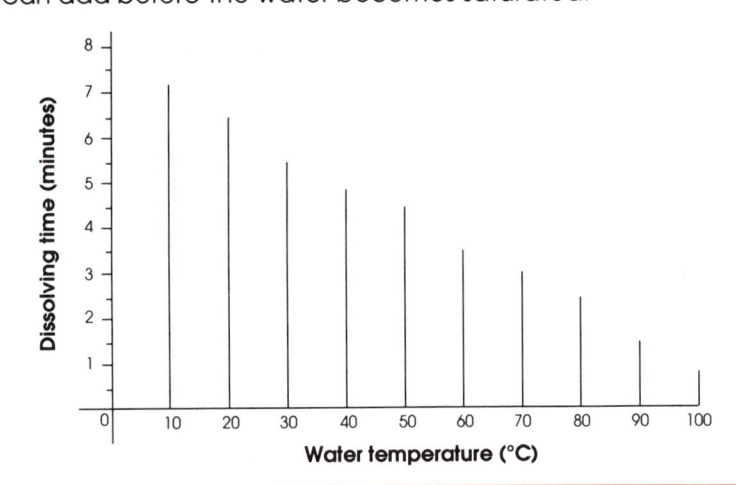

> ⚠ Very close supervision is needed if water over 50°C is used. An adult should demonstrate any dissolving in boiling water. The children may suggest heating the mixtures. An adult should do this. The materials suggested are safe to heat.

Science background

When sugar dissolves in water, sugar and water molecules mix to produce a solution. The water is the solvent because it dissolves the sugar. The sugar is the solute.

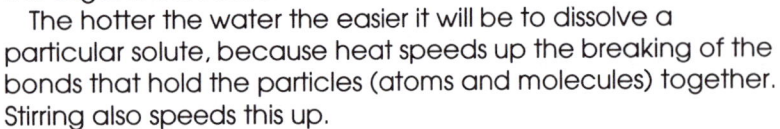

The hotter the water the easier it will be to dissolve a particular solute, because heat speeds up the breaking of the bonds that hold the particles (atoms and molecules) together. Stirring also speeds this up.

Dissolving is a complex process and depends largely on the type of bonds between the atoms and molecules as well as the molecular sizes involved. A solution is said to be 'saturated' when no more solute will dissolve in the solvent.

Assessment

- Did the children check that the spoonfuls were the same size?
- Did they work out ways of making their test more reliable (for example, weighing the samples)?
- Did they ask questions that could be tested?
- Can they think of everyday uses for solubility, for example sugar in tea, the difference between instant and leaf tea?

IDEAS BANK - Materials and Change © Folens

Solubility

Which of these materials will dissolve in water: salt, sugar, washing powder, sand, instant tea ?

You may need...
- salt
- sugar
- washing powder
- instant tea
- sand
- a spoon
- plastic beakers
- a timer

Investigate...

- Half fill each beaker with cold water.
- Drop a spoonful of salt into one beaker.
- Time how long it takes to dissolve:
  – with stirring
  – without stirring

Record...

- Record your findings on this graph:
- Which materials did not dissolve?

S = stirred
N = not stirred

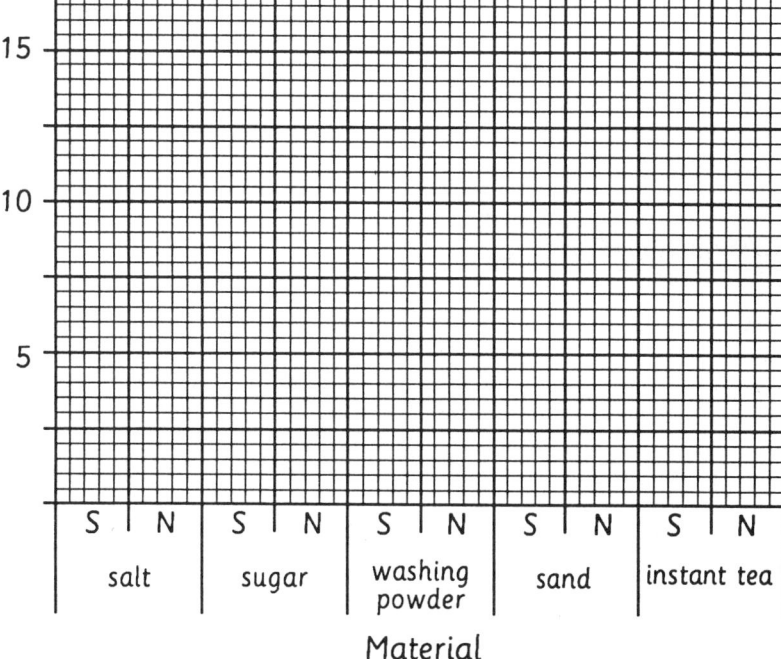

Now...

- Find out what difference it makes if you use hot (not boiling) water.

© Folens — IDEAS BANK - Materials and Change

Evaporation - Ideas Page

Purpose and context

Understanding
- Evaporation is part of the water cycle.
- It describes a change of state from water to water vapour.
- Evaporation is a physical change.

Skills
- Repeating observations and measurements to improve reliability.
- Using results to draw conclusions.

Questions
- What happens to rainwater on a sunny day?
- In what sort of weather does washing dry the quickest?

Investigation

Activity page
- Ask the children to explain why the water level in the uncovered pot has gone down.
- Display their theories.

Theories shown:
- The fairies could have drunk it
- Someone could have knocked it over
- it soaked through the pot...
- ... then it soaked through the shelf.
- it just dried
- The sun dried it

- Ask them in groups to plan a fair test to find out if one of the theories is true.

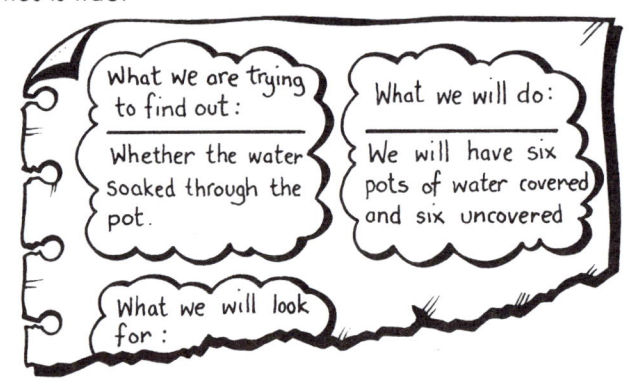

Planning sheet:
- What we are trying to find out: Whether the water soaked through the pot.
- What we will do: We will have six pots of water covered and six uncovered
- What we will look for:

Science background

During evaporation water changes from liquid to vapour without boiling. Molecules of water from the surface move into the air. This process is speeded up if there is wind.

Water cycle diagram:
- Rain falls and is soaked up by land, also producing mountain streams and rivers.
- Water travels from high to low ground and into the sea.
- Clouds move over the land
- Evaporation of water

Assessment

- After the investigation ask the children again to explain their ideas about where the water went to.
- They could compare their new ideas with those displayed.
- Have they changed their minds?
- Did they repeat any tests as part of their verification process?

IDEAS BANK - Materials and Change

Evaporation

Where does the water go?

You may need...
- plastic jars
- foil
- a rubber band
- a marker pen
- a measuring jug

Investigate...

- Put the same amount of water in the two containers. (They must be the same size and shape.)

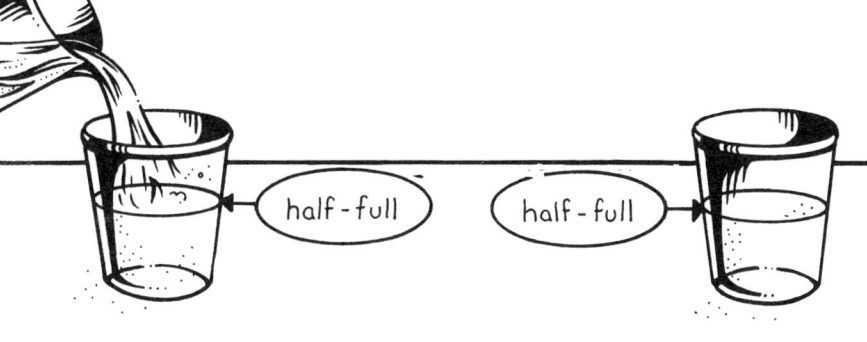

half-full   half-full

- Cover one with a piece of foil. Secure it with a rubber band.

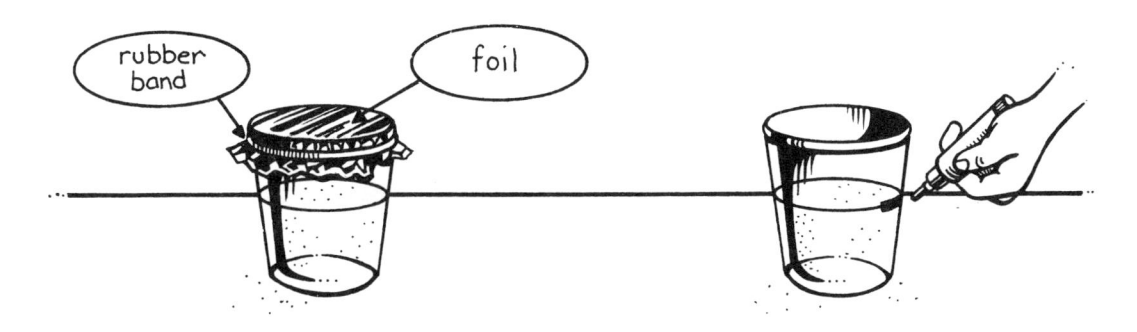

rubber band   foil

- Mark the level in each jar.
  Put them on a sunny windowsill for 2 days.

Record...

- Draw a set of diagrams and notes to show what has happened.
- What do you notice about the water levels? Explain this.

Now...

- Try out the experiment again. Do you get the same results?

© Folens   IDEAS BANK - Materials and Change   25

Sieves - Ideas Page

Purpose and context

Understanding
- Solid particles of different sizes can be separated by sieving.

Skills
- Turning ideas and questions into a form that can be investigated.
- Using predictions to aid planning.
- Making observations.
- Using simple equipment.
- Using results to draw conclusions.

Questions
- When do you use sieves at home?
- What materials do you separate at home using sieves?
- Why do some sieves have larger holes than others?

Investigation

Activity page
- Provide a selection of sieves from which the children can choose the most appropriate for their investigation. Some should have large holes, for example garden sieves. Also useful are colanders, wire sieves, nylon sieves and tea strainers.
- Draw the children's attention to the sizes of the holes in the sieves and the sizes of the solid particles to be separated.

⚠ *Warn the children not to taste any of the food materials used.*

Development
- Can the children apply what they have learned to different contexts? Ask them to design a process to separate coins of different denominations. Can they use their ideas to explain how slot machines separate coins?

Science background

Sieves and filters (see pages 28 and 29) work in the same way. The difference is that sieves have holes that are visible to the naked eye, whereas filters have tiny holes that can usually only be seen using a microscope.

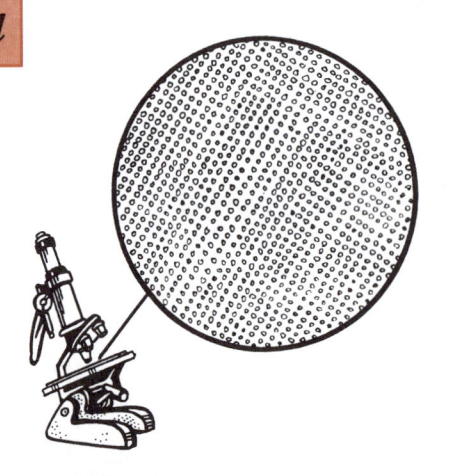

Assessment

- When selecting their sieves, did the children take account of the sizes of the particles to be separated, or did this have to be pointed out?
- Could they explain how a sieve works?
- Can they relate this to everyday use of sieves, strainers and garden riddles?

IDEAS BANK - Materials and Change

Sieves

What materials can a sieve separate **?**

You may need...
- a collection of sieves
- sand
- salt
- dried peas
- large plastic pots
- large stones

Investigate...
- How can you use a collection of sieves to separate sand, salt, dried peas and large stones?

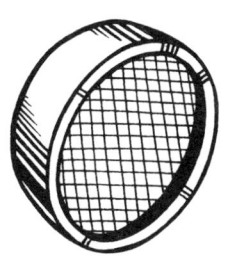

What we will do.

What we will use.

Predict... What we think will happen.

Record... Our findings.

Interpret...
- How do sieves work?

Now...
- How can you separate materials that are too fine for a sieve to separate?

© Folens   IDEAS BANK - Materials and Change

Separating and purifying - Ideas Page

Purpose and context

Understanding
- Insoluble solids can be separated from liquids by filtering.

Skills
- Using simple equipment.
- Making observations.
- Repeating tests for accuracy.
- Using tables to present results.
- Using results to draw conclusions.
- Explaining conclusions.

Questions
- What everyday uses do people have for filters? (Washing machines, dishwashers, cars: oil and air filters, coffee machines.)
- Which of these filters separate solids from liquids?
- How do they work?

Investigation

Activity page
- The children should make each mixture themselves before filtering it, so that they are aware of what has been mixed with the water.
- Chalk, sand and mud can be filtered out of water, because they do not dissolve.
- Sugar and salt cannot be filtered.

Our filter papers: Chalk, Sand, Salt, Mud, Sugar

- The children could record their results by displaying the labelled filter papers.

Science background

Filters can only separate undissolved solids from liquids, since dissolved solids become part of the liquid. Their particles (molecules and atoms) combine with the liquid to form a new material. The tiny holes in the filter paper allow the liquid to pass through but not the solid. A filter is really a sieve with very tiny holes.

Assessment

- Can the children use the results of the investigation to decide whether or not a substance is soluble?
- Can they distinguish between 'melt' and 'dissolve'?
- Ask the children to describe what some everyday filters do: what do they separate from what?

Separating and purifying

How can you separate a mixture **?**

You may need...
- filter papers
- salt
- a funnel
- water
- a plastic container
- sand
- sugar
- muddy water
- powdered chalk

Investigate...

- Mix a solution of chalk and water.
- Pour it through a filter.
- Examine the liquid at the bottom of the container.

Record...

- Record your results on the chart below.
- Now try other mixtures.
- Repeat each test to check your results.

Mixture	What was left in the filter?	What was in the container?
chalk		
sand		
salt		
sugar		
muddy water		

Now...

- Find a way to separate salt from water.

© Folens   IDEAS BANK - Materials and Change

Separating a mixture - Ideas Page

Purpose and context

Understanding
- Solid particles of different sizes can be separated using a sieve.
- Insoluble materials can be separated from liquids by filtering.
- Some metals are magnetic and can be separated from a mixture using a magnet.
- Dissolved solids can be separated from a liquid by evaporating the liquid.

Skills
- Using predictions to aid planning.
- Selecting equipment.
- Using simple equipment.
- Making observations.

Questions
- How can people remove the salt from sea water?
- How do people stop tea leaves getting into their tea cups?
- How do people keep coffee grounds out of their drinks?

Investigation

Activity page
- Iron filings will rust after exposure to water. Any small iron or steel items are suitable, for example used staples.
- Ask the children to consider the best order to carry out each separation: sieving, filtering, evaporating, using a magnet. Their predictions will be helpful during this process.
- Magnets should first be wrapped in tissue paper secured with sticky tape, otherwise iron filings will be difficult to remove.

① A coarse sieve removes gravel

② Filtration removes sand and iron filings

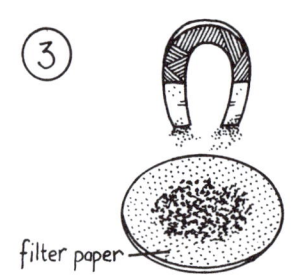

③ A magnet removes iron filings from the sand

④ Evaporation separates the salt and the water

Science background

Gravel and sand are different-sized solid particles and so can be separated using a sieve. Sand can be filtered from water. Salt dissolves and must be separated from the water by evaporation. Iron filings and sand have solid particles of a similar size, as do staples and small grain gravel. Steel and iron are magnetic and so the steel or iron items can be separated from the gravel or sand using a magnet.

Some materials do not dissolve in water even if stirred vigorously or heated. Dissolving depends largely on the type of bonds that hold together the atoms and molecules of the solute and also the molecular sizes involved. The molecular structure of the solvent is also a factor (see page 22).

Assessment

- Did the children realise that they needed to sieve the mixture first to remove the gravel?
- Could they separate the iron filings and sand from the salt water using filtration?
- Did they use their knowledge that salt dissolves?
- Did they use a magnet to remove the iron filings?

Separating a mixture

How can you separate a mixture of gravel, sand, iron filings, salt and water **?**

We may need...

- Use this page to plan and record your experiment.

Investigate... What we will do.

Predict... What we think will happen.

Record... Our findings.

Interpret... What we learned.

Now...
- How could you improve your investigation?

Solid, liquid and gas - Ideas Page

Purpose and context

Understanding
- Recognising differences between solids, liquids and gases.

Skills
- Making observations.
- Using tables.
- Making comparisons.

Questions
- Which foods are solids? Which are liquids?
- How do you eat liquid foods?
- How is this different from the way you eat solid foods?
- Which foods have gases in them?
- How can you tell?

Solid	Liquid	Gas
chocolate	lemonade	bubbles in lemonade
apple	orange juice	air in bubbly chocolate
potato	tea	air in candy floss
sugar	coffee	
salt	soup	

Investigation

Activity page
- The children's observations will reveal their understanding of the terms solid, liquid and gas.
- Ask them how they know that something is solid. Use words such as hard.
- Draw attention to whether materials stay in one place, or keep their shape when removed from a container.
- The children should notice that liquids can be poured, but not in the same way as solid particles such as sand.

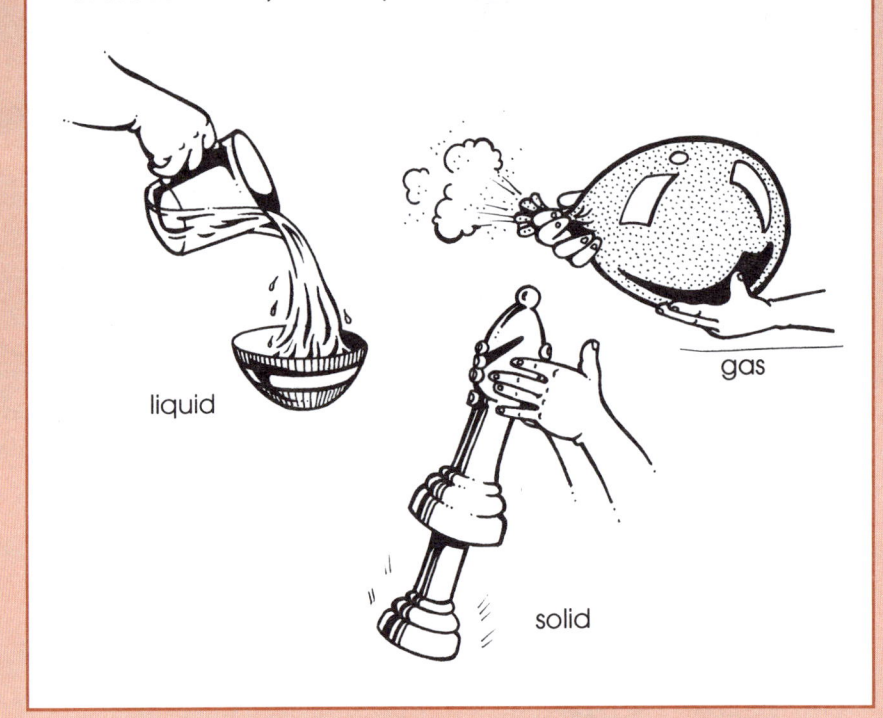

liquid

gas

solid

Science background

The physical state of a material depends on how the bonds that link its particles (atoms and molecules) are behaving.

Solids keep their shape when removed from a container because their bonds hold the particles firmly together. Liquids move about more freely because their particles, although joined, allow movement. The particles of gases are not held together, allowing the material to move in any direction. Because their particles are further apart than those of liquids and solids they can be compressed, as when air is forced into a balloon.

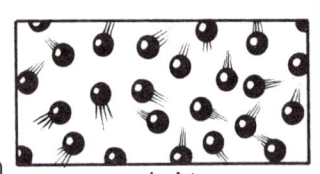

Solid

Liquid

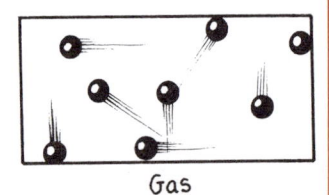

Gas

Assessment

- Do the children notice that solids keep their shapes?
- Do they notice that liquids move about, can be poured and take on the shape of their containers?
- Do they notice that air escaping from a balloon moves about freely and escapes in any direction once released?

IDEAS BANK - Materials and Change

Solid, liquid and gas

How do you decide whether
materials are solid, liquid or gas?

You may need...
- freedom to look around

Investigate...

- Sort these materials into the correct places on the chart.

sand    water    ice    air

honey    jelly    ice lolly    cola    bubbles

Solids	Liquids	Gases

- Add some more of your own.

Interpret...

- How are the solids alike? _____

- How are the liquids alike? _____

- How are the gases alike? _____

Change of state - Ideas Page

Purpose and context

Understanding
- Pure water is liquid at temperatures above 0°C and below 100°C.
- Water changes from liquid to solid at 0°C. It becomes ice.
- As water freezes it expands.

Skills
- Turning questions into a form that can be investigated.
- Using predictions to aid planning.
- Measuring temperature.
- Recording measurements and results accurately.

Questions
- How does ice damage walls and pipes?
- How can people prevent pipes freezing in winter?
- How is a freezer different from a fridge?
- What everyday liquids become solids when left overnight in a freezer?
- Can you think of any that will not freeze?
- How do people prevent the water in car radiators freezing in winter?

Investigation

Activity page
- Ask the children to describe what happens to water as it becomes colder.
- They may say that it freezes or turns to ice, but ensure that they appreciate that this is a change from liquid to solid.
- Draw their attention to the lids of the tubs. Can they explain why the one from the freezer has lifted up?

Development
- Can the children predict at what temperatures water will boil and ice will melt?
- Provide each small group with a pot of crushed ice and a thermometer.
- Demonstrate, using a kettle or pan over a heat ring, the changes that take place as water boils.
- A glass pan allows the children to see what is happening without getting dangerously close.
- The children could record the temperatures on line graphs.

! Use spirit filled thermometers (usually containing red or blue liquid). Mercury is poisonous.
Take care when handling containers from the freezer. Use gloves or a cloth to prevent 'ice burns'.

A graph to show the temperature change of melting ice

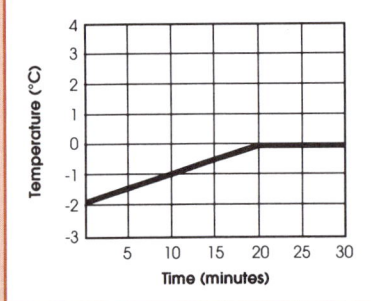

A graph to show the temperature change of water that is heated

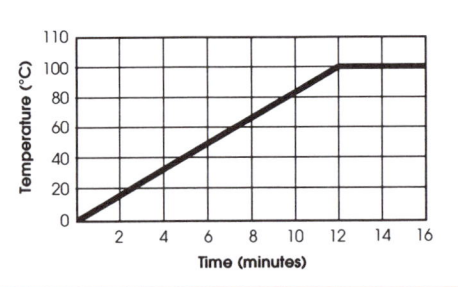

Science background

Changes of state: liquid to solid and vice versa, solid to gas and vice versa take place at constant temperatures. Ice with no impurities melts at a constant 0°C at atmospheric pressure. The temperature, contrary to many children's expectations, does not rise until after melting has taken place. Similarly, pure water maintains a constant 100°C as it boils. It cannot have a higher temperature than this.

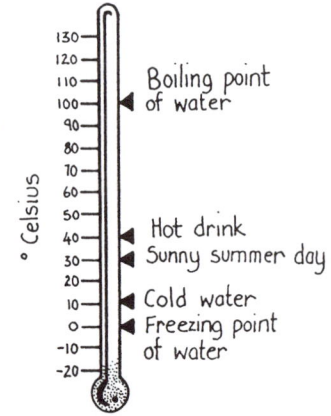

Boiling point of water
Hot drink
Sunny summer day
Cold water
Freezing point of water

Assessment

- Do the children understand that freezing means a change of state from liquid to solid and that boiling means a change from liquid to gas?
- Can they name the solid and gaseous forms of water?

Change of state

What changes take place as water becomes colder?

You may need...
- two plastic ice-cream tubs with lids
- a freezer
- a fridge
- a freezer thermometer
- a room thermometer

Predict...
- How low does the air temperature have to be for water to freeze?

Investigate...
- Fill the tubs to the top with water.
- Put one in the fridge and the other in the freezer.
- Leave them overnight.

Record...
- Record any changes.

Air temperature	
in the freezer	°C
in the fridge	°C
in the room	°C

Water in the fridge: _____

Water in the freezer: _____

- Try changing the setting of the freezer (Get permission!). Repeat the investigation.

Interpret...
- Explain your findings.
- What is the highest temperature at which water will freeze?

Insulation - Ideas Page

Purpose and context

Understanding
- Materials that feel warm are usually good insulators of heat. They help to keep cold materials cold and warm materials warm.

Skills
- Fair testing.
- Using predictions to help in planning.
- Using simple equipment.
- Making accurate measurements.
- Recording results.
- Interpreting results.

Questions
- How do people keep cold foods cold when travelling to a picnic or transporting them to shops?
- How do people keep soup and coffee hot when travelling?

Investigation

Activity page
- Ask the children to feel a collection of materials.
- Can they arrange them according to how warm they feel?
  Coldest feel ▷ warmest feel.
- During the investigation shown on the activity page, encourage the children to keep the test fair by using similar amounts and thicknesses of each material.
- The children could record the temperature of the hot water at the start, then every five minutes.
- Results could be recorded on a line graph.
- The children could leave ice cubes, wrapped in different materials, for an agreed length of time (about 20 minutes), then unwrap them and compare the size of the unmelted ice.
- Draw their attention to the feel of the good insulators.

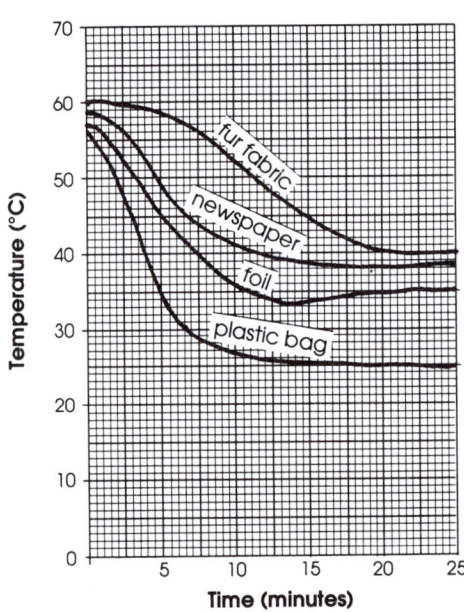

Science background

Metals feel cold because they are good conductors of heat. They conduct heat away from the hand that touches them, making it feel cold. Warm-feeling materials, such as expanded polystyrene, feel warm because they are poor conductors (good insulators). They do not conduct heat from the hand. The temperature of the inside of a large block of polystyrene may actually be colder than the air temperature, because the material is such a poor conductor of heat that the inside takes an extremely long time to change to match the temperature of its surroundings.

Assessment

- Did the children realise that the same materials that keep things cool can also keep things hot?
- Did they notice that warm-feeling materials are good insulators?
- Could they explain this?

IDEAS BANK - Materials and Change

Insulation

Which materials are good insulators of heat **?**

You may need...
- an ice cube
- a drinks can
- hot (not boiling) water
- a thermometer
- fur fabric
- newspaper
- foil
- timer
- a plastic bag

Predict...
- Which material will be best to wrap an ice cube in to stop it melting?
- Which will be best to keep water in a can hot?

Investigate...
- Plan a fair test for your predictions.

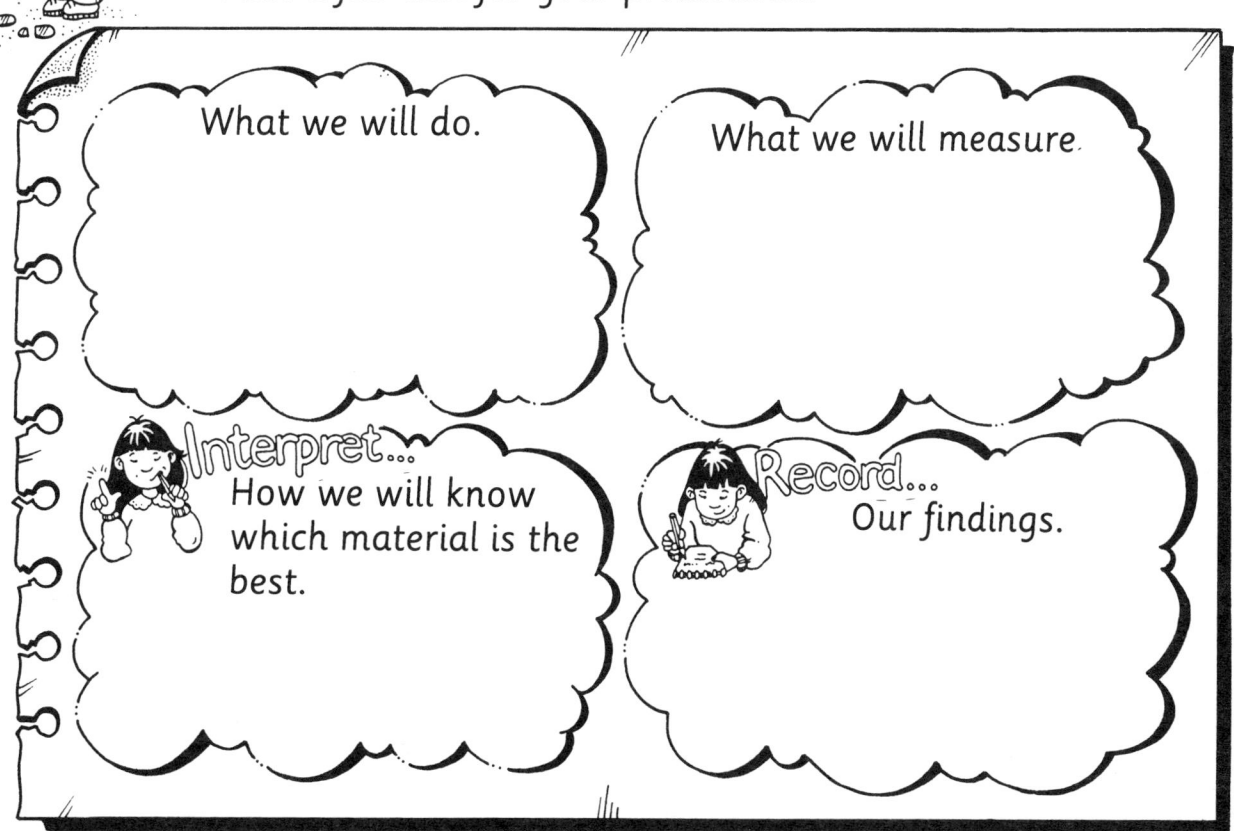

What we will do.

What we will measure.

Interpret...
How we will know which material is the best.

Record...
Our findings.

Now...
- Check your results.
- What conclusions have you drawn?
- Explain any surprises.

IDEAS BANK - Materials and Change

Melting chocolate - Ideas Page

Purpose and context

Understanding
- Some solids become liquid when heated and change back into a solid when cooled.
- Heat can change the state of materials.

Skills
- Using simple equipment correctly.
- Using results to draw conclusions.

Questions
- Which everyday materials melt when heated?
- Why do we keep butter in a fridge in the summer?
- What happens to tarmac on a hot day?

Investigation

Starting point
- Let the children examine a solid bar of chocolate – and eat some!
- Discuss what might happen if the chocolate is left on a sunny windowsill.

Activity page

! *All equipment should be sterilised. The children should wash their hands, wear aprons and tie back long hair. Close supervision is essential. The water need not be boiling.*

Development
- Ask the children to pour liquid jelly into different-shaped containers. They could find out which takes the longest to set.

Science background

It is important not to confuse melting and dissolving. Dissolving happens when solid materials combine with liquids. Melting occurs when a solid is heated and changes into a liquid.

dissolving — melting

Melting is linked to an input of energy such as a rise in temperature.

Most solids are denser than their liquid form. Ice is an exception.

The melting point of a substance is the temperature at which it melts or changes from solid to liquid.

Assessment

- Do the children realise that some solids melt when heated and then become solid again when cooled?
- Can they think of things that might melt in the sun, such as ice cream and butter?
- Can they describe what happens to materials when they melt?

IDEAS BANK - Materials and Change © Folens

Melting chocolate

You may need...
- a bar of chocolate
- a small bowl
- a large bowl
- cornflakes
- hot water

What happens to chocolate when it is heated **?**

Investigate...

- Break up the chocolate and put it into a bowl.

- Stand it in a pan of hot water, until the chocolate melts.

> ⚠ Work with an adult. Do not have the water dangerously hot.

- Mix some cornflakes into the melted chocolate.

- Put spoonfuls out on to a baking tray and let them set.

Predict...

- Describe what you think will happen when the chocolate has cooled down. Will the shape change? Why?

Record...

- Write a recipe for cornflake cakes.

Now...

- Try heating other solids such as jelly, sugar, salt, flour, butter. What happens?

© Folens   IDEAS BANK - Materials and Change

Cooking an egg - Ideas Page

Purpose and context

Understanding
- Heat changes an egg.
- This is known as a chemical change.
- It cannot be reversed.

Skills
- Fair testing.
- Making observations.
- Using simple equipment safely.

Questions
- What foods do people boil? Why?
- How do foods change when they are boiled in water: rice, chick peas, cauliflower?
- What are the different ways that you can cook an egg?

Investigation

Close supervision is essential.

Activity page
- For a fair comparison the eggs should all be the same size.
- Draw attention to the changes in the yolk and albumen (white): colour, texture, change from transparent to opaque. Compare these changes with those that take place when chocolate, butter or ice are heated. (These are reversible – no new material is produced, just a physical change – solid to liquid.)

Development
- Can the children think of anything else that would change permanently when heated? They could make cakes, scones or biscuits and make careful observations of the changes.

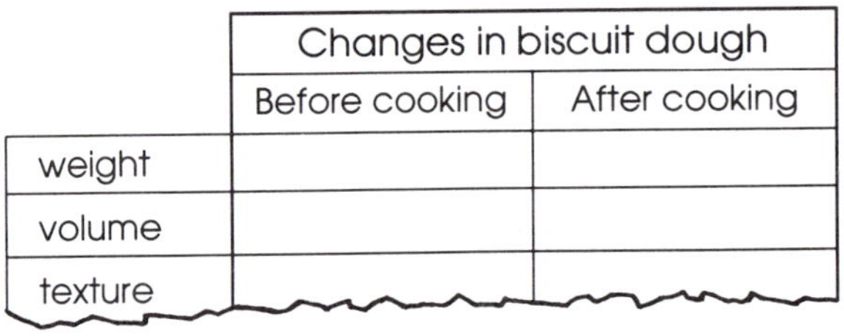

	Changes in biscuit dough	
	Before cooking	After cooking
weight		
volume		
texture		

- Cook eggs in different ways: scramble, poach, omelette. Beat egg whites and record the changes over time. The children could record the permanent changes made to eggs by heating in different ways, or beating.

Science background

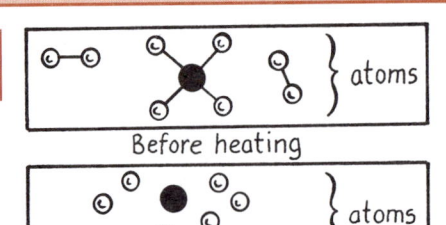

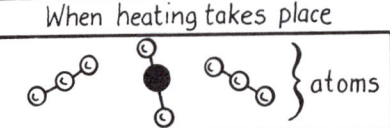

When a chemical change takes place the particles (atoms and molecules) of a substance separate from each other. The bonds that hold them together break. The particles re-combine differently, making new bonds. A new substance is formed.

When an egg is boiled it undergoes a chemical change in its state. Heating changes the proteins in an egg. The shape of their molecular structure changes.

Assessment

- When describing an egg in its raw and boiled state (after different time intervals), did they notice the transparency/opacity, colour and hardness?
- Did they think of weighing and measuring the eggs?
- Were their timings accurate?

Cooking an egg

What happens inside an egg when it is cooked **?**

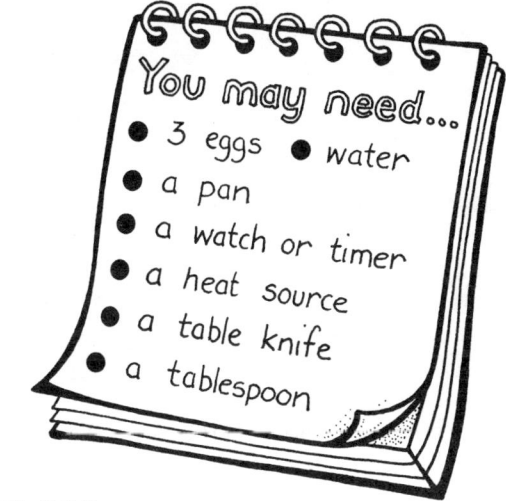

You may need...
- 3 eggs
- water
- a pan
- a watch or timer
- a heat source
- a table knife
- a tablespoon

Predict...
- What happens when you cook an egg for 2 minutes, 6 minutes and 10 minutes?

Investigate...

⚠️ Work with an adult.

- Boil some water in a pan.
- Put in an egg, leave it to cook for 2 minutes.
- Open it up.
- Repeat the experiment, cooking an egg for 6 minutes and 10 minutes.

Record...
- Record your findings on this chart:

Cooking time	Was the yolk liquid or solid?	Describe what the egg looked like when it was opened
2 minutes		
6 minutes		
10 minutes		

Interpret...
- Could you change an egg back to its original state?

Now...
- What happens to other things when they are boiled in water? Do they become softer or harder?

Candle change - Ideas Page

Purpose and context

Understanding
- A change takes place when a candle burns: solid to liquid to gas.
- There is less wax after burning because wax is the fuel that is burned.
- This change is not reversible.
- When wax is heated, not burned, it becomes a liquid. This change is reversible.

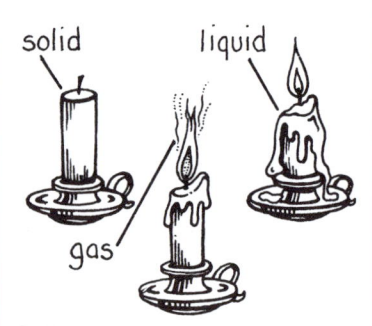

Skills
- Turning ideas into a form that can be investigated.
- Using predictions in planning.
- Deciding what evidence to collect.
- Using simple equipment correctly and safely.
- Using charts.
- Using results to draw conclusions.
- Evaluating results against predictions.
- Explaining conclusions in terms of scientific knowledge and understanding.

Questions
- What materials are burned as fuels?
- How do they change during burning?
- Can they be changed back to how they were?
- What fuel does a candle use as it burns?

Investigation

Activity page
- Record the children's predictions on the chart provided. Their predictions should reveal their existing understanding of materials used as fuels, and change of state.
- They may need to draw their own charts to record their findings. Draw attention to the colour and physical state of the wax while it is hot.
- Ask the children what happens to the wax. Is there as much after burning as there was before? Where has it gone?

Development
- Let a few drops of hot wax fall on to a cool saucer. Ask the children to watch what happens as the wax cools.
- Dropping hot wax into a bowl of cold water has an even more spectacular effect.
- Draw the children's attention to how the wax has changed when heated and when cooling. How is this different from when the candle burned?

! It is important that this activity should be carefully controlled by an adult. Point out that flames can be dangerous.
Ask the children to devise their own safety rules. They could consider the reasons why Plasticine, a foil tray and sand are included in the equipment list. Ask them to think about clothing, hair and their movements.

Science background

Chemical changes take place when a new material is formed. They are not easily reversible. Physical changes take place when a material changes from solid to liquid, liquid to gas, and so on. When a candle burns, oxygen from the air and wax from the candle combine to produce energy in the form of heat and light.

Assessment

- Do the children realise that melting wax is a change that can be reversed, as is melting ice to make water?
- Do they understand that burning is different from melting in that the wax is converted to energy to provide light and heat?
- Did they think of weighing the candle before and after burning it?

Candle change

What happens to a
candle when it burns ?

You may need...
- matches
- a candle
- Plasticine
- a foil dish
- sand

⚠ Work with an adult.

Predict...
- Describe what will happen to the after the candle has burned out.

Predictions

	Before burning	After burning
Colour		
Feel		
Weight		
Size		
Shape		

Investigate...
- What will you need to do before the candle is lit?
- Set the candle up as shown here.
- How will you make sure of safety?

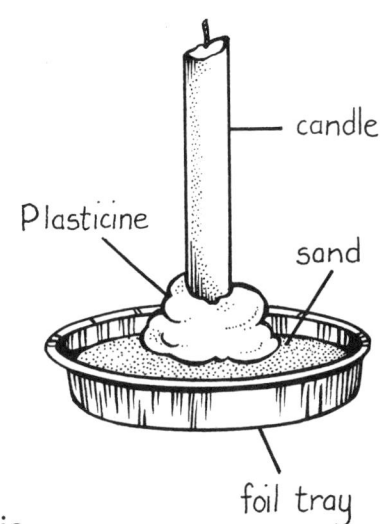

_____

_____

(Diagram labels: candle, Plasticine, sand, foil tray)

Record...
- Ask an adult to light the candle.
- Record your findings on a chart like this:

Wax	Before burning	While burning	After burning
Colour			
Feel		Do not feel or weigh a burning candle.	
Weight			

Interpret...
- Explain what has happened to the wax.

© Folens — IDEAS BANK - Materials and Change

Cooking - Ideas Page

Purpose and context

Understanding
- Mixing materials, such as flour and water, can cause them to change.
- Heat can make ingredients combine, making a new material (non-reversible change).

Skills
- Fair testing.
- Turning questions into a form that can be investigated.
- Deciding what evidence to collect.
- Using simple equipment safely.
- Observing and measuring.
- Using results to draw conclusions.

Questions
- How do foods change during cooking (appearance, weight, moisture)?
- Can any foods be changed back to how they were before cooking?

Investigation

Activity page

⚠ *Close supervision is essential. If the childen are to taste the 'dampers', ensure that the conditions are hygienic. Equipment should be washed in hot water. The children should wash their hands and tie back long hair. Hair should be covered.*

- The two kinds of dampers mentioned on the activity sheet are typically eaten by the Bushmen of Australia. They can be cooked over an open fire and improved by adding a little baking powder.

Science background

Heat causes the particles that compose the materials (flour, water, egg and milk) to separate from each other and re-combine to form a new material. At the same time water from the mixture evaporates. If baking powder or self-raising flour are used, bubbles of carbon dioxide form. These bubbles make the mixture rise.

baking powder added

mixture rises due to formation of carbon dioxide bubbles

Assessment

- Can the children explain the difference between changes during cooking and changes during melting?
- Do they know which changes are reversible and which are not?
- Do they realise that loss of moisture causes the weight loss from raw to cooked state?

IDEAS BANK - Materials and Change

Cooking

What happens to flour and water when they are heated together **?**

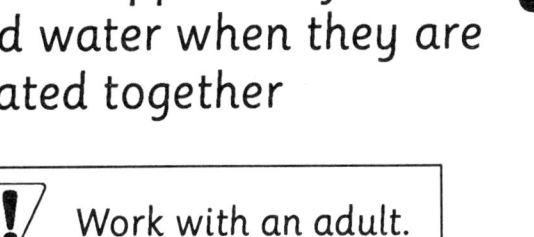

You may need...
- plain flour
- water
- milk
- an egg
- a tablespoon
- an oven
- a mixing bowl
- a timer or watch
- a baking tray (greased)

⚠️ Work with an adult.

Investigate...

- Make 'Australian dampers'.
- Mix 10 tablespoonfuls of flour with enough water to make a dough.
- Shape and bake the 'dampers' for 20 minutes at 220°C.

Share a baking tray with friends

Record...

- Compare the raw and cooked dough.

	Raw dough	Cooked dough
Weight		
Size		
Feel		
Appearance		

Interpret...

- How has the dough changed?

Now...

- Find out what difference it makes if you mix the flour with egg and milk instead of water.

© Folens — IDEAS BANK - Materials and Change

IDEAS BANK SCIENCE: Materials and Change

Knowledge and Understanding of Science:

Materials and their properties

Use these pages to assist in the assessment and recording of children's progress in both knowledge and understanding and in scientific investigation.

Pupil Record: Knowledge and Understanding of Science

Child's name_____ Date of birth_____ Class teacher_____

Scientific concept	Assessment: teacher's and child's comment
Can sort materials into metals, textiles, wood, ceramics, plastics, skins.	
Can distinguish between natural and manufactured materials.	
Can explain why drainpipes are often made of plastic.	
Notices that some plastics are denser than others and that some are more fragile than others.	
Explains how a metal is different from other materials.	
Can distinguish between common metals by observable characteristics.	
Knows that brass and copper are not magnetic and that iron and steel are magnetic.	
Knows that iron and steel rust when exposed to air and water.	
Names some common materials that decay quickly: paper, fruit, wood, leaves.	
Understands that hardness means resistance to scratching.	
Explains that sand and gravel are mixed with cement to increase its roughness.	
Knows that cement irritates the skin. Appreciates the need to protect the skin.	
Names some common materials that dissolve in water.	
Uses a filter to separate undissolved solid matter from water.	
Names some everyday materials that are solid, liquid or gas.	
Knows that the freezing point of water is 0°C, and its boiling point is 100°C.	
Knows that the same materials that keep hot water hot, also keep ice cool.	
Explains that when puddles of rain dry up, the water moves as small droplets into the air.	
Knows that a baked cake is lighter than an uncooked mixture because water evaporates during cooking.	

Many of the activities provided in this book are introduced in a way which allows the children to reveal what they know about the concept. If they are made aware of this both before and after scientific investigations, they are involved in their own assessment – they know what they have learned. This will be more apparent to them if their written ideas before and after teaching are compared, and perhaps kept with the assessment record.

ASSESSMENT

Experimental and Investigative Science

i. Planning experimental work
ii. Obtaining evidence
iii. Considering evidence

Skills

i)
  a. Turns ideas into forms that can be investigated.
  b. Uses predictions in planning.
  c. Decides what evidence to collect.
  d. Understands how to control the factors affecting an investigation.
  e. Considers what equipment and materials to use.

ii)
  a. Uses simple equipment correctly.
  b. Makes careful observations and measurements.
  c. Repeats observations and measurements to check them.

iii)
  a. Presents results using bar charts, line graphs and tables.
  b. Makes comparisons and identifies trends or patterns.
  c. Uses results to draw conclusions.
  d. Tells whether the evidence collected supports predictions.
  e. Tries to explain conclusions in terms of scientific knowledge and understanding.

Pupil Record: Materials and Change: Experimental and Investigative Science

Child's name_____ Date of birth_____ Class teacher_____

Skill	Page	Example	Assessment comments: teacher/child
i) a	20–21	Decides that the toughest cement mixture means the most difficult to break.	
i) b	22–23	Predicts which solids will dissolve in water.	
i) c	20–21	Decides to measure the height from which cement mixtures smash when dropped.	
i) d	22–23	When planning a test to find how stirring affects dissolving, notes that the same amount of water and solid must be used each time.	
i) e	36–37	Selects a thermometer, equal-sized drinks cans and equal-sized pieces of fabric when testing insulators of heat.	
ii) a	36–37	Uses a thermometer correctly.	
ii) b	10–11	Compares the strength of fabrics by counting how many 'rubs' on an abrasive surface are needed to make a hole in the fabric.	
ii) c	28–29	Repeats, for accuracy, tests to separate mixtures.	
iii) a	8–9	Uses a chart to show the properties of different plastics.	
iii) b	34–35	Notices that while water is changing from solid to liquid or liquid to gas its temperature remains the same.	
iii) c	44–45	Concludes that baked dough is lighter than the uncooked mixture because water has evaporated from it.	
iii) d	10–11	Uses the record of the number of rubs needed to make a hole in each fabric to decide which is the toughest.	
iii) e	14–15	Explains that steel cans are coated with steel because steel rusts, but aluminium does not.	

Please note that these are only examples of the many occasions on which these skills may be used during the activities presented in this book and, for assessment purposes, others may be substituted here. The assessment panels on the teacher pages provide suggestions. In each of the activities skills of scientific investigation are not practised for their own sake only, but are used by children in developing their understanding/knowledge of science.

© Folens

8 ways to help ...

There are many ideas in this book about developing and extending the photocopiable pages. Here are just eight ways to help you make the most of the **Ideas Bank** series.

1 Paste copies of the pages on to card and laminate them. The children could use water-based pens that can be wiped off, allowing the pages to be re-used.

2 Put the pages inside clear plastic wallets. They could be stored in binders for easy reference. The children's writing can again be easily wiped away.

3 If possible, save the pages for re-use. Develop a simple filing system so that the pages can be easily located for future use.

4 Use both sides of the paper. The children could write or draw on the back of the sheet, or you could photocopy another useful activity on the back.

5 Make the most of group work. Children working in small groups could use one page to discuss between them.

6 Photocopy the pages on to clear film to make overhead transparencies. The ideas can then be used time and time again.

7 Use the activity pages as ideas pages for yourself. Discuss issues and ideas with the class and ask the children to produce artwork and writing.

8 Customise the pages by adding your own activities. Supplement the ideas and apply them to your children's needs.

IDEAS BANK - Materials and Change © Folens